A TRIP to the FIREHOUSE

A Grosset & Dunlap **ALL ABOARD BOOK**®

To Kevin P. Williamson

Special thanks to the entire staff
of the Falmouth Fire Rescue Department in Falmouth, MA,
and to all the children.

Library of Congress Cataloging-in-Publication Data

Lewison, Wendy Cheyette.
  A trip to the firehouse / by Wendy Cheyette Lewison ; photographs by Elizabeth Hathon.
    p.   cm. — (All aboard books)
  Summary: A group of school children visit a fire station and learn how firefighters do their jobs.
  1. Fire stations—Juvenile literature. [1. Fire stations.] I. Hathon, Elizabeth, ill. II. Title. III. Series: Grosset & Dunlap all aboard book.
  TH9148.L48   1998
  628.9'25—dc21
                                                        97-41109
                                                               CIP

ISBN 0-448-41740-5   B C D E F G H I J   AC

A TRIP to the FIREHOUSE

By Wendy Cheyette Lewison
Photographs by Elizabeth Hathon

Grosset & Dunlap, Publishers

David and his class are visiting their neighborhood firehouse today. That's why David is wearing a special shirt. It's fire-engine red!

The fire chief himself greets the children at the door. "Welcome to our firehouse, girls and boys," he says. "We have lots of exciting things to show you."

He lets everyone try on a real fire helmet.

Next they meet the firehouse dog. The children guess his name. They guess right—it's Spot!

The firefighters tell them that Spot has not eaten his breakfast yet. Would they like to come inside and feed him?

YES, they would!

While Spot is eating, the children look around.

David sees the firefighters' gear on one wall. Three firefighters show how long it takes for them to put it all on. Less than thirty seconds!

Katelyn finds the firehouse
pole. "Hello-o-o, down there!"
calls a firefighter way up at
the top. He grabs the pole
with his hands and legs,
and slides down—*whoosh!*

The pole is an important part of the firehouse, he explains.
It helps the firefighters move fast when the alarm rings.
It is much faster than going down steps. When there's a fire,
every second counts!

Josh points to the hole in the ceiling. "What's up there?"
he wants to know.

"You can see for yourself," says the firefighter. He leads the children upstairs.

They see where the firefighters sleep. There's a bed, a lamp, and a locker for clothes.

There's even a bed for Spot.

There's a kitchen, too, where the firefighters can make themselves something to eat—and maybe share exciting stories when things are slow.

Next the children are taken to see the dispatch room. Things are never slow here!

It is busy all day and all night. Computer monitors flash. Telephone switchboards ring. It is here that phone calls come in, telling operators where the fires are.

Some calls come from 911, the number many communities use for emergencies.

It is here also that alarms come in.

An operator shows the children how the system works. Someone spots a fire and pulls a lever on an alarm box. That makes this bell clang—right here in the firehouse!

The bell clangs a certain number of times, in a pattern or code. The code is punched out on this tape, so it can be seen and recorded.

The operators look up the code on this big blackboard—
to find out which alarm box the alarm is coming from. Then
they know exactly where to send the fire trucks.

Different kinds of fire trucks do different things. Some help at forest fires. Some help at fires in tall buildings. They carry different kinds of special equipment.

Many of these fire trucks are kept at other firehouses. But all are in perfect condition, ready to go, whenever and wherever they are needed.

Duty Officer's Vehicle

Heavy-Duty Rescue Truck

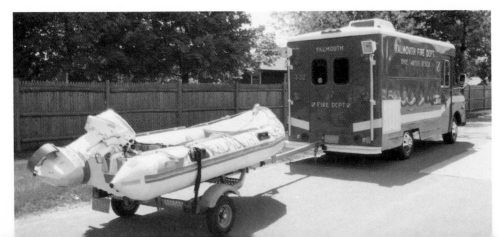

Dive/Water Rescue Truck

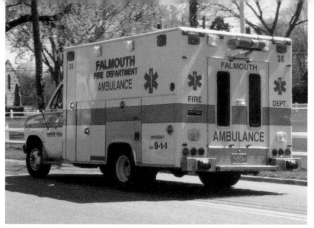

Ambulance

Brush Breaker

Fire Chief's Car

Aerial Ladder Truck

The children go downstairs now to get a good look at a
fire truck that is kept at this firehouse. They climb all over it,
outside...

...and inside. They pretend they are real firefighters, steering the big engine down the streets of town...

and calling the dispatch room on the two-way radio.

They examine the bell that clangs, the siren that screams...

the hoses that whoosh, the valves that click.

Everything needs to be kept in perfect working order.
All the parts need to be checked, and checked again.

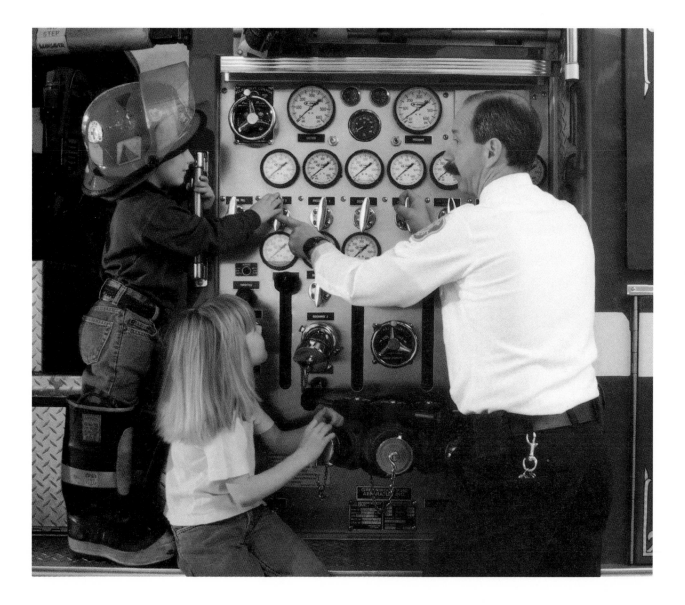

The fire truck needs to be clean, too. And since it's such a nice day today, the children are invited to help. They soap it up...

...and rinse it off.
Everyone has fun.

Spot has fun, too, playing ball with one of the firefighters!

When the children are done with the washing, they help
a firefighter roll up a long, flat fire hose. Katelyn thinks it
looks just like a snail!

Then the rolled-up hose is stored on the truck with other
hoses—ready to use at a fire.

The firefighters tell the children they've done a great job.
They deserve a special treat...

...bagels and cream cheese in the firehouse kitchen! Yum!
The firefighters and the children are just finishing up their snack, when—*clang! clang!*—the alarm rings!

In a flash, all the firefighters get up and rush out of the room.

Down the pole! Into their gear!

The children watch out the window while the firefighters scramble onto the fire engine.

Off they go down the street. *Whoo-ee! Whoo-ee!*

The children wave. They are sorry their visit to the firehouse is over. But they know the firefighters have a big job to do.

They hope this fire can be put out fast. And most of all, the children hope they are invited back to the firehouse soon!